The National Poetry Series was established in 1978 to ensure the publication of five collections of poetry annually through five participating publishers. Publication is funded by the Lannan Foundation, the Amazon Literary Partnership, the Poetry Foundation, Barnes and Noble, the Gettinger Family Foundation, Bruce Gibney, HarperCollins Publishers, Stephen King, Newman's Own Foundation, News Corp, Anna and Olafur Olafsson, the O. R. Foundation, Laura and Robert Sillerman, Elise and Steven Trulaske, Amy R. Tan and Louis De Mattei, the PG Family Foundation, the Betsy Community Fund, and the Board of NPS. For a complete listing of generous contributors to the National Poetry Series, please visit www.nationalpoetryseries.org.

2016 COMPETITION WINNERS

I Know Your Kind
by William Brewer of Brooklyn, New York
Chosen by Ada Limon for Milkweed

For Want of Water
by Sasha Pimentel of El Paso, Texas
Chosen by Gregory Pardlo for Beacon Press

Civil Twilight
by Jeffrey Schultz of Los Angeles, California
Chosen by David St. John for Ecco

MADNESS
by Sam Sax of Austin, Texas
Chosen by Terrance Hayes for Penguin Books

Thaw
Chelsea Dingman of Tampa, Florida
Chosen by Allison Joseph for the University of Georgia Press

THAW

thaw

POEMS BY CHELSEA DINGMAN

The University of Georgia Press *Athens*

Published by the University of Georgia Press
Athens, Georgia 30602
www.ugapress.org
© 2017 by Chelsea Dingman
All rights reserved
Designed by Erin Kirk New
Set in New Caledonia
Printed and bound by Thomson-Shore, Inc.
The paper in this book meets the guidelines for
permanence and durability of the Committee on
Production Guidelines for Book Longevity of the
Council on Library Resources.

Most University of Georgia Press titles are
available from popular e-book vendors.

Printed in the United States of America
21   20   19   18   17   P   5   4   3   2   1

Library of Congress Cataloging-in-Publication Data

Names: Dingman, Chelsea, author.
Title: Thaw : poems / by Chelsea Dingman.
Description: Athens : The University of Georgia Press, [2017] |
    Series: The National Poetry Series
Identifiers: LCCN 2016056639 | ISBN 9780820351315 (pbk. : alk.
    paper) | ISBN 9780820351308 (e-book)
Subjects: LCSH: Families—Poetry.
Classification: LCC PR9199.4.D565 A6 2017 | DDC 811/.6—dc23
    LC record available at https://lccn.loc.gov/2016056639

for my father

This is how it continues:

The cold, the snow, the slight trembling in your hands.

—Daniel Simko, "Homage to George Trakl"

Contents

Acknowledgments

Grateful acknowledgments to the following editors and the presses where these poems first appeared:

The Adroit Journal: "Letters from a War"
burntdistrict: "The Suicide"
Dialogist: "For My Son: A Forest of Stars"
The Fourth River: "After the Tornado: Summer 1989"
Carolina Quarterly: "Amid Reports of a Blizzard & Black Ice on the Coquihalla Highway" (formerly, "Clan of Fatherless Children") and "Hands, I've Had"
Grist Journal: "Hunting" and "The Gulf"
The MacGuffin: "Hiraeth"
Milk Journal: "Sunset" and "When My Mother and I Speak about the Weather"
Mom Egg Review: "Dog Days"
Raleigh Review: "The Windsurfer" and "Any Other Sun"
Red Sky: Poetry on the Global Epidemic of Violence against Women: "Sirens"
RHINO Poetry Journal: "Little Hell"
Slipstream: "Ancestry" and "Hungry Season"
So to Speak: "Current" and "Elegy for My Child"
South Dakota Review, "Daughter, Released"
Sou'wester: "Sirens," "Woman, Disarmed," and "Burning"
Stone Highway Review: "Billy"
Vermillion Literary Journal: "From a Morgue in Minnesota"
Yemassee: "Felled Pine"

I want to thank Hunter and Sawyer for being so patient, even though these words took me away from them while I was in the same room. Laine and Shelby, thank you for always making the trek across worlds to see me. I may be gone, but I'm never far. To my mother: though we don't always agree, thank you for what you've given me, for the years you struggled. You taught me the resilience of women.

Also, thank you to the amazing writers and mentors to whom I am indebted: John A. Nieves, not only for helping me to conceive of myself as a poet but for helping me turn this project into a book. Also, for always believing. I owe you everything. Jay Hopler: without your teaching and guidance, this book would never have been written. You made me the poet that I am. "Thank-you" is too small a word. Rita Ciresi, Ira Sukrungruang, Heather Sellers, John Henry Fleming, Karen Brown, and Jarod Rosello: thank you for everything. I was lucky to be part of something great. To my cohort at USF: thank you for giving me your eyes and your words.

I want to thank Allison Joseph for believing in this work, for her praise, and for making this wild dream a reality. I am also incredibly grateful to the National Poetry Series, its donors, and Beth Dial, who was a great support in this process. To the University of Georgia Press: thank you for making books, for making this book, and to each person I worked with, for this wonderful experience. I couldn't have asked for better.

To my husband, Chris: this was all your idea, and I'm making the most of it. Thank you for giving me this chance, for the endless laundry and grocery shopping that you've done while I've been away. You made this possible.

And to my father: thank you for the years we had, too few, but ingrained in me all the same. For a few minutes, each time these words are read, you are alive in the world.

1.

PROOF OF DISAPPEARING

Hunting (circa 1985)

What we grieve is
not how death can be
dispelled in a photo, or a dream
on our hip we carry
like a child. But a man's eyes,
blackened by the butt of a rifle.
Stars fading in the crosshairs
of the sun. A phantom
trigger, his finger
hooked through its heart.

At a glance, the blood
could belong to a deer, breath
escaping in the chill fall
air, just smoke.

Like the camera, our eyes fail
to see what falls outside
the frame—twisted limbs
like a bird's wings
broken on the ground. How a bullet
can enter so quietly as to leave
a skull almost intact. How,
afterwards,
a body glitters
like the cherry
still burning
in someone else's fingers.

From a Morgue in Minnesota

Ataxia Telanglectasia is a rare, neurodegenerative, autosomal
recessive disease causing severe disability and appears in early
childhood.—A-T Children's Project

We bury a child each year, sometimes
two, bones like cell bars, bland food

fit only for a baby's slick gums. Their mothers
wait years for a chest to flutter

closed, herringbone ribs
barely lining the canvas. False

light, a shaft, hangs children
in moving hands like miners

digging six feet down. Each child
withers—an anorexic who refuses

water, heart protesting
long after the body is lost

hope in our mouths. Crowning,
they wrap their hands in a fist. Then,

at age three, they can't. Bodies turn
inward, a flower's petals folding

regardless of the rain, tender
ground, the unwavering desire

that forces our eyes away.

Felled Pine

Behind black curtains, dogwood
blossoms scattered from seam to seam, I
asked after you, a secret

squirreled away like a moment
I can no longer see. Children
crying in the wet street, you pretended

to control the rain, a ruse
to ease our fear. I wonder
where you'll wake this morning, sickness

sticking to your skin. We didn't
drag you to the nearest bed, stay until the fever
broke. It's what I'd do if you were my child,

but you are the sibling
four years behind me, tiny scars
we carved into our arms like names

in wood, little hearts. I always thought
you'd age, rings on an old pine
in a churchyard in Revelstoke, soft

and rotting from its cuts, bark crumbling
beneath my fingers. But you lost yourself
in the sky, ruined by years

of rain and snow, dirty
hands on the saw before you fell.

Sirens

Say someone will come, but no
one comes. The echo

filters through buildings, palm fronds
feathering tile and stone,
                    yet I remember

only mountains, snow circling our house
like crows' wings. How I long for the metal

sting numbing my hands. I had
a mother then. I held the wind
in my throat like a song. A coal-

black sky, blue-lit by morning
that arrives too late, somewhere
north. I lay down on the bed to sirens

   like a loon's calls. Like a warning. The torn pocket
   of skin dangling where the blade exited

my mother's back. Each staple
making a new hole. Tonight,
no one comes

         with sounds that carry, with water
that will tumble from the sky. That starved town
in the distance is the gash

where she was torn from
breast plate to shoulder

blade. If I could unzip cold
skin, maybe I'd know
how to stop reaching

    for snow, dark blue
    mountains haloed by stars.

Little Hell

I can't breathe this
morning—my dead father, smoking
at the kitchen table, marred

by the scenery, trees
on the flatbed of his truck
going somewhere. He's

a terrible dream I had. Empty
rooms, dust in a corner. He
disappeared near Hope, ice

beneath his tires, and I
went south, to vultures
feeding on entrails

in the yard, dead
armadillos. I escaped
the snow, not its secrets. They follow,

whispering of mold
in the grass, corpses
of trees, naked and shivering.

Testimony of Hinges

This is how we stay: tongues
on fire, two people dancing
to our own screams. This is how

we dance: you, on the phone,
begging to come back to a house
I flee on foot. To the dagger

in my mother's smile. This is how
you love: fingers trawling the skin
under my shirt as I pretend to sleep. If not me,

who else do you skin? My father
sleeps in a body I can't touch. You are someone new
who abandons hair on our pillows, the day

turning us against ourselves. If I leave
now, no one will know
I broke my wrists to give you my hands,

sawed clean through the bone. I dreamt
new hands, pink-tipped fingers
to drag over the knobs of your spine. All I have left,

dear stepfather, is my mouth: a blade
I draw across the petals of your flesh, bruised
blood rising in ragged blooms.

Athanasia

This body is in tatters, worn
by winter's long argument
with the snow. Perhaps it's time

      to speak of rusty hinges:
your eyes closed while you sleep,
hands steepled, a pale mouth's

flattened horizon. Violet sheets
swell the space
you once lay next to me

in the dark. It comes to this: a shudder
in your chest, my breath
seeking a warm place where

there is only a body
of snow. The words I hold back,
you can't have now. But on this skin's scroll,

      we wrote with our hands, words
that can't be ruined by cold,
empty streets, a second hand. Perhaps we are gods

now, black ink spelling us out—
new blood threading the bodies

of the damned.

Elegy for Empty Rooms

There will be no more sons. Bodies
twisted in the shade
of a canopied crib. I know

the shape of their blood, the long
wait for their faces
to materialize. What exists now

behind a closed door? In me, a hollow is
ice-cold. I exist to exist, a street
covered in snow. I dreamt

more faces at dinner, the table
stretched by wooden wings. Instead, I endure
parlor games: at a party, a chain

dangling over my navel, pressed flat
as a penny. How the chain spins, then
stills. How stillness tells me

I'll only know spring's passing
as a field somewhere
the skies are all red.

Dog Days

I can't stop the dawn
to catch my breath. You expand
while my eyes rest, as if you're taking

on water. I'm unsure of your best
interests, so vast, your childhood
is a foreign country, this language

I struggle to master. An accident
is in the street up ahead
unless each mile is driven

with careful attention
to the signs, an eye
on the highway behind. I drive

to follow you, it seems, rather
than little steps I remember
at my heels. My burden

is a landmark, a turn.
Your life becomes the road
away. The quiet sores I carry.

Amid Reports of a Blizzard & Black Ice on the Coquihalla Highway

The forecaster says it will snow
and I tell my son *yes* when he asks
for waffles, peanut butter. I can't mention
your truck in a gully
somewhere. How we used to sling songs
into the night, windows
rolled down. I didn't know you were close
to death. That my cupped hands waited
only for what falls. I want
to tell you everything. How my greatest fear is leaving
my child behind. How, afterward, I ran from the world
like snow from the sky. They say snow is harmless,
yet I know what it is to be lost
when touched. There is so much I want to say to you,
but I choose to stay quiet like the stars
amidst the sky's falling. I choose to live.
The weatherman keeps talking and I wait
to hear him say there's been a crash. For you
to sprout wings from your back
on the side of a road. I wait
in this room with my son. The world
outside, obliterated. Only we are left, less
whole. The walls are winged
beasts that fold themselves over us.
You are the snow.

After the Tornado, Summer 1989

Like a branch felled
from the oak in our front yard, hunger harkens
my spine, stretched

   toward the sky. For a mother, I'd kneel
all day. I'd go back: the trailer
park, empty hands, palsied

bodies waiting for something
else. I wait when there is no one
to tell me how to lay down again,

to sleep. I scratch the mud-
soaked earth with a stick until it bleeds
water. Until it covers every inch of skin

I can muster. Some women
carry children over mountains
on their backs. I do the walking.

I learn how to fall. Behind
closed eyes, I can't see
the sky's struggle, dust

made of the dead. Mothers, many times,
bear more than one heart-
beat. But, my mother's breath is

misplaced somewhere. The broken
leg on the last chair
left at the table, only I can know

I live like this windswept plain:
because the sky is done
                    starving.

After the Accident

You told me you'd be
here. The restaurant fills

and refills, yet dozens of faces
are not yours. Heat from the kitchen

reaches glass doors
where I stand waiting, a fog

so thick it reminds me of the forest
when we used to sneak out

at night. We couldn't see anything: the moon,
pine needles like thousands of tiny fingers.

As I wait, I wonder if you were playing
when you fell. The week before

last, we sat on the roof amidst the stars
as if we belonged to the sky,

bright and unbidden. You wanted to feel
the night become otherwise. Please know, little

brother: I watched over you like a reflection, skin
sealed by old bruises. Still—they say

your palms were burnt, a star
caught in your throat. I came here, tonight,

to keep a promise. To tell you
I can no longer see

the pines, a stitch
of moon through their fingers.

To the God I Prayed to as a Child:

are you working against us
children's eyes and hands
unfurling like petalled wings
little bones bare
flanked in blue flannel
plastic bands printed with their births
they curl on their sides
they wither—and you stay away
from wet lips spitting your name
ribs petalling closed around a breath
the sun that rises anyway
is this silence a sign? if it were crimson
I'd know to stop speaking
does their stalled breath make an enemy
of you? I'm tired of putting my faith in
the skin's pinked surface a ceiling
of sky that never fails to surface
the clouds' dirty gutter after a murderous rain
I won't lie I've had enough waiting
while you push against us
without showing your hands [sigh] I've had
enough of your petty tricks   I'll save myself
for someone else tonight

Erebus

Sometimes you slip inside
my skin without an invitation.
Maybe it's my own need

to forget the sounds of night
pulling away, your fingers
shining like precious stones

on a distant sky. Some lives are like this:
four heads at the dinner table,
a fable before bed. Why now,

do I long for someone new? Is it because
you're like the dark tide, manipulating
sand? My chest stings shut, collecting our bones

too great a task for the earth, silver
night. How do I trust myself to go underground
with you, a region railed by wind? I want different seasons,

yet I favour fall's dark days, lost leaves,
the trees' bare bodies untouched
by any other sun. Leave behind the chaos

you come from, a fierce wind
hugging your ribs. We made someone
once, our bodies sewn together

only to part. The mouth
of a god bellowing
in the bed between us.

Onshore Years Later

Water wells below all surfaces and, yet,
everything on the surface
looks whole. My father's lost

skin, an olive veil I pull
over my body when I want to
remember. His voice

stains my tongue. I want to know how
I sound, lips pressed against an ear
at dusk, drunk

with sun-fall. A shadow
drags its knuckles along the Gulf. This sea
is not the sea I was born to. Does water

return or escape? From a pier, swimmers
spill themselves into the sea
between breaks. I hold what remains

of my father, grainy between my fingers,
and imagine his blue eyes, burning. In my fists,
I begin to unfasten ashes

from my skin, salt
from the sea, the grave
way we drown.

On Nights When I Am a Mother

Lord, make these black waters blaze,
bolted down, a bright beam
to which I'm bound. Make me an ocean

to empty into, limbs and wombs and ash-
black plumes speaking of night
somewhere else.

I can't own this world, clenched
in your closed fists. Can you

hear me on my knees? It that you: rain
rising in the gutters, the moon's scaly skinned head,
the cough caught in my son's throat?

I encircle his body, lungs racked
with fluid, wondering which of us you'll save
from drowning.

The hush of your hands buries me
in sleep's calm dark. Will you come for him
as you came for my father, before

I'm ready? Wrapped like petals around
his slim shadow, I hold tightly, as if you won't be able to

pry him away with a hammer and a crowbar.
With a gasp of your blazing breath.

Prayer of the Wolf

Forgive these fangs. How I kneel
for nothing anymore. Retreating rock ruins
my knees, elbows bearing the scarlet bloom
of roses running ramshackle over
a wooded hillside. I have only scars. Above,
the sky is so clear. Should I have to beg
to remain that way? Your name, the growl
in my throat, I confuse you for a friend in the dark
and gentle snow. Snow savages a man
somewhere in the distance, a last twitch
as his cheek hitches itself to unfailing
eyes. The sky still so clear. How quickly
we become something else. Is it wrong
not to kneel when I know the snow
will fall anyway? Behind the walls
of every wood, a child. This girl is no more
a little girl as winter kicks a hole in the sky. I'd howl
your name, but it sounds like a saw
to the skinned pines. Please tell me
where you go when cows low
in the fields, bellies dragging over tall grass,
black soil. Night falls and you take the moon
out of its tin cage, only to parade it
before us. I beg you—the hours
want nothing except to reclaim themselves. I
have hunted you like the white
moon, yet I'm lost. I hear bleating,
but it leads me further away
from the sky's clenched fist. I long for
wool, rubbing against my limbs, bloody as the slain
body in the snow. What can I hope to become
when a lone lamb can't be salvaged
and hunger is all I have?

Sunset

Do you forget the roar
of tiny lungs unsettling
your sleep? How I was once, a sparrow
lost in the yard? Or was it safer
for you to let him
open new seams, your scars still
so raw? I used to wake
and run all of the faucets,
as if we lived inside the falls. The house, lit
like a constellation. Was I ever yours
after that? There is such violence
in the sunset. You wanted me
to beg, but I held my breath as I wanted
to be held. I should have said I wanted sky
to claim the stars. That I understood
to be a good girl I had to lie
low like the aging hardwood floor. But, when I return,
it's to stand in the soft light
on the sun-porch. To admit the sunsets
are drawn by my hand.

Woman, Disarmed

Above flat grasses, red
skies like a torn dress. The streets pass
without returning. Unknown,
now, who will call you
mother & sister &
daughter before
you're the expanse of milk-
weed & memory under our tongues? Tell God
you prefer green. How it brings
out your eyes. Is your body
the prayer, skin
peeled back to reveal the pearls of
your knuckles? Like children,
I want to line your promises
along a wall, take
measure. Where you go,
fields may be fallow. Yellowed
and shorn. But the bow
you left to me.
Abandoned building, I look through
shattered windows
to learn what life
you gave up. I remember
night, taunting me
into your room. The light I crawled toward
like a war. Is this mercy?
Reckless world, held captive
inside a snow
globe. Our beauty,
in the shadows:

the drawers we kept
shut, moving shapes
not yet named. I don't want to know
how your voice fails, the shadow
that will hold you
apart.

Hungry Season

I asked for a demonstration
of faith, not a ring or ceremony

built on strange words. A ritual
that only we would know—song

written on a sleeve, body
glowing against the late afternoon, silky

with sweat, shutting out noise
rising from the street. I wanted

a promise to carry like a stone, smooth
between my thumb and forefinger, days

when you fell away, and I couldn't feel
the heat on my skin. We are

the secret I hunger: old initials
on a sidewalk after the sun

sealed our prints together, proof
your hands once ached mine.

Daughter, Released

You empty from my body like a song
on the radio that ends
right after I find the station. Then,
a different song. I dream you
in a pink frothy dress, curls
wicked around your ears. I wake
and the house is silent,
save for the cries
behind every door. Is there no end
to the dark's wanting? There was once
a child, before snow melted
inside my bones. Before
I could say I wanted to be
a mother. How few seconds it takes
to be otherwise. Outside, snow
climbs metal siding. The sun, white
like a dandelion as it's dying. I try to whisper
Go into the wind, as if you will
listen. They tell me
you weren't ready, but I fear
they mean me. That I have to find
what comes from darkness
before anything good can stay.

Billy

For my father

You wear a little girl's shoes, laced
over the ankle, in the picture dated
1963, waiting for your father to come

home from the fields, already drunk,
three-year-old daughter under a makeshift
cross of sticks behind a tree swing. Lips

and teeth nasty brown, tobacco tucked
in his gum, you wanted to join him,
not knowing when he made you quit

school, you'd pay for the son before
you, stillborn, carrying the weight
of extra place settings, your mother's

arthritis tying her to a chair, watching
disease ebb at him, ninety pounds. He
gave his last nights to a dog, instead,

licking his cold bones to sleep.

Waiting for Winter's End

Why did you bring snow
to cover the pavement's grey
beaded coat? I drive past
lilies' petals petrified by cold
licking their smooth skin. You aren't

beyond the glass sky, a blue mountain's snow-
filled mouth, the slithering creek on its belly.

Can I get some direction? I call your name,
out of the car, snow crushing my crown,
wind threading water. Is that your fingers
dripping blood? Aren't we all
your children? Lost on this road:
low hanging sky, inked water
split by silver-shelled stones, the moon's
scarred face. O, how can I trust in
the things my eyes can't see?

Even in the dark, sun-spoiled glaciers empty
into a stream.

If the red sun refuses to rise soon,
I'll know you can't salvage any of us,
winter's dark hands at our throats.

Borderlands

You hop in your pickup, drive south
to Spokane, Seattle, places
you'll need a gun at camp. Not to hunt
deer or elk, but to pretend at being young

boys again. You don't stop
at the town you grew up in. You only know
how to want: a house somewhere
new, somewhere you can stretch

and storm. Aren't we also the road's
lure: three kids around the kitchen
table, swing set in the yard? You want
to leave long before you load the flatbed,

September's teeth in my mother's
knees. Which one of you understands
sacrifice? Her nights spent at a motel,
cleaning filthy sheets. You, driving

the TransCanada highway, black coffee
in hand, windows unrolled. But my mother
doesn't yet know she will be a widow,
raising us alone. By the phone, she waits

to hear about a house you've found
us, the day she'll get to own something
for the first time. You could leave her
before your truck swerves. She's still

young, daydreaming about a new dress
to wear out with her friends. Instead,
you don't have to grow older, see the mess
you left on the highway outside town.

Hit and Run

Ahead, taillights disappear
    like pieces of a red dress shirt. His body

lies to the left of twisted yellow lines,
    a god who has fallen
        too far from sky. You kneel, small

coin of your ear covering a mouth, smoky
    breath leaking into the night. Your son,
        framed by the window at your back,
            tells you not to go, not to

bend and break
    like waves around a beach. Not to bear the weight
        of another man's prayers.

        His black pupils.
    Your slowed breath.
        A single set of headlights
            shining. The sky and the ground: two black seas.

Traffic streams somewhere beyond the scene. Brakes squeal
            like the body that flew, not a bird with wings
    but a man fallen before you. Is it a comfort
        that his eyes can't look away? Flashing

lights and sirens crush the blacktop, a last hymn
        that means nothing to you, a body
            more bird than god. The wind,
    like breath, unburying its heart.

The Suicide

There are birds, pedaling
through the open-throated
morning, the sky
still flushed. A horn, sirens,
in the distance. But not rain.
Just mist, burning off
like a woman disrobing: first
one shoulder, then
the whole. The birds,
black-feathered, circle
slowly, as if they hang
suspended by invisible strings.
On the ground, something
damaged—tied together, beaten,
pieces of collar and coffin

bones. Does the animal's
name not matter anymore?
They land, attendant. But only
after it seems there is no
movement. Should this dark
creature roll over, suddenly,
hoarse with pain, the birds
would flee for the trees
like children caught in a
strange house. Like sirens,
chasing something lost.
Not like bodies, mid-fall,
wings tucked close at their
sides. Following sound,
not a beast that can still rise.

Immortality

Wind hollows the wheat
chaff, howl of a stray
hungering morning. This terrible north
collects pieces you don't
recognize. Your mother, grey
two-story house, singing
through a distant night, *lay down
your sweet head*. Outside
the chapel, under a streetlamp,
you draw a picture of God
in the snow, where He isn't
merely a man, lost
in this human hour, body
weeping in the thaw.

In Ten Years

My mother forgets she's a mother,
voices trickling down a drain
in a lockdown ward. She waits
for people she no longer knows, sandpaper
skin scaly and weathered. Her bags
packed at her feet each morning, I hold her
hands, put her clothes away.
She calls me by her sister's name.
Her body, another country
tarnished by dry winter air.
South of her borders, I suffer
the loss of my children's tiny bones,
high voices. At my mother's greying
house, we're kind strangers, no history
hiding in the corners of the room. She's lost
as a forest of pines are lost: one tree cut
from it's roots, then another, naked
patches of ground dotting the mountainside.
In these spaces, I find her: young,
before my father didn't make it
home. Before motherhood
buried her under record snowfalls.
My eight-year-old feet skip
to school through the woods, skirt
willowing in the glacial wind. Her eyes
follow, turn
away.

In the Absence of Sky

The trees shiver. When my neighbor calls me
to the woods, summer idles
on the street. The sun, bare-lidded. I am

a new game under his gaze.
It isn't until he folds both knees
in fallen leaves that I notice

the sky, missing. Only the oaks' arms fly
overhead, a canopy of green. Wind swells
through us like thunder. I can't focus on

anything but the absence of blue,
the forest's edge. Longing to run,
I stand still, arms thrust high

above. His voice is soft and
trembling, but I can't refuse
the storm creeping in like dark

wallpaper. The crows circle,
borrowing heat from the earth
below before day's

end. Perhaps, as children, we are only
spared by degrees—the water's
depth, a storm's brute

force, the hands willing
to unspool branches,
to let light in.

While He Is Missing

There is a door
        in the dream

for him to enter
the way water enters

        the body,
but doesn't stay.

He smells of cigarettes
and coffee, of vodka and the forest's damp

musk coiled in his hair. Smoke
   is the only thing to escape

his mouth. You wait to hear
if the end sounds like rain

running through the trees, praying
not to hit hard ground—

to find shelter, instead, in a body
of water that lays bare

across land. Look—
he sways in the inches

stretched between shadows. His name,
        dancing

on your lips like broken shutters. You leave him
like this each time: a father. Stranded

    in a place where nothing can forgive
                the coming rain.

Another Genesis

A tribeswoman, now: my mother is
the summer sun, resting her body
on the flat-backed sea. She slips

slowly below the water line, as my otherness
grows. Long ago, we belonged. Without warmth,
I shiver as she submits—yellow bones

braiding the sea, a blurred sky's wings
wavering in the wind. Will anyone see the sky
without the sun? What will water become

without a body stretched blue
to reflect? No one prepares for this
wound. A daughter can't know how to stop

reaching. The water ripples
at midday: a pair of cerulean skies. I can't see
the way I came to be here. A tribe of stray bodies surfs

the shore, waves dragging themselves
through sand. Sun-bare, I wait for night
to unnail her body from the sea.

The Last Place

A few hard drops strike
soil. Petrichor rises and I can't
remember how far away
you lived. Years become galaxies. You are not
with me, as people suggest. I haven't felt you
anywhere but where I saw you last,
so many skies from here. Who holds a child's memories,
now that I am no longer a child? Some man
made of clouds and wind, perhaps. Or maybe
it has been you all along, rolling them
like cigarettes in your fingers: days
at the lake, in the cab of your truck,
singing on the highway as trees flee
our speeding bodies. As stars
hitch themselves like flags
to our tailgate in a blue night.

Ancestry

You squeeze your eyes shut
on the Rockies, as if you could ever forget. Water

threads itself through land, blood
beneath the skin, always in danger

of spilling. You wear this place.
The heavy snow. Sorrowing sky. Wildfire

burning your nostrils. It is woven
in your psyche like a tattoo. A reminder

of wanting. The past,
another child you carry on your hip,

needing nurturing. Years
thin, blood left

on bending highway, reeds,
pine trees hunted and skinned, white

of their bones raking the sky—
undone. Dense pine

forests outlast withering frames, fragile
temperaments. They will not die

with you. You carry them south, roots
still buried in the Columbia River valley, yet growing

in your marrow all the same, moss
over knuckles like decaying stumps, thick

scent of earth bringing you home.
At midnight, afraid, you talk to wind, missing

bodies, places that fathered you.

Letters from a War

After another man's name
    found your mouth, after
        the bodies laid down

until they couldn't rise, after
    I began to see men
        as streets and mountains

and moving skies—I starved
    just enough to stay
        hungry. Not to kneel

before deep voices, reaching
    for any word that didn't
        force its way into my mouth. Why

is my body still empty
    with another inside? I used to think
        I'd go thirsty to see you

break like a highway's bones
    under the winter snow. Maybe
        mornings you forget braiding

thick bundles of hair over
    old bruises. But I've forgiven
        how your whispers sound

like regret. How a mother leaves
    when the night is long. My belly brims
        with someone, slight and soundless,

who I can't refuse. I know now
  how briefly we are beautiful. How the first
    death, for women, is our own.

2.

PROOF IN DISAPPEARING

Epilogue to Drowning

You rub your thumbs
between my shoulder blades, a lie
in each stroke. How did we get here? The first time

you feathered my skin
with your tongue, I decided to drown.

I didn't want our limbs to ever break
the surface of water, indecent
sky. But, I'm not sure anything can be done

now. My body can't outrun your fingers,
falling like flames. At my back, new

wings—open doors of my ribs
spread wide to expose kidneys,
a heart. When your hands travel

these wounds, will your cuticles catch
like blades? I never thought

it would come to this: two people undone
by their hands, open
mouths. Our downfall will not be

emptiness, darling boy, but the water
we dare to fill our lungs.

Winter in the Rockies

Is this heaven? Hidden
highways. An avalanche. Nothing
around for miles to hear tires
leave the road. The mountains
bow, back-lit by white skies. I walk
& wonder if I walk for any reason
except to walk. My father,
drenched in drifting snow, was left
here. Yet I can't say I'm closer
to the truth about loss than I was
as a child when the world I saw
was a world that doesn't ache
to be anything else. It's funny
how easy it is to forget
the sound of water in winter. I lay down
on the banks alongside the frozen
lake. Its long body, still. But
I'm listening now, as water
like a sleeping child wrestles
with the blankets pulled over
its face, waiting to see
which one of us will wake.

Athena

When I last saw him, he could've been
anyone's father. The good daughter, dragging him
from snow banks in a dream, his black hair

curled in my fingers. His hair hadn't had time
to grey. I turned him over. Put my mouth to his,
tasted diesel fuel, a blazing tail-

pipe between my lips. My feathers,
fallen at our feet. Awake, I stand
on a four-lane highway, canyon

walls like crows' wings
curling over a creek. No sign of snow
that held him in its white womb

until he was someone else. His mouth
is not mine but one my son wears
to kiss me goodnight, to tell me

the dark is only a temporary lapse
between bodies: earth and sun,
a god and the child he armours.

Prayer for an Unnamed Child

Tonight, I'm empty, a Ford
pickup stalled at the lights,
the shoulder of town, thin-skinned
streets bare of any sidewalks. A plea

scorches the night's black-stitched ear,
licked dry by daylight. Perhaps

it is only tires that shriek,
the pavement's gasp,
glass on the road.

I stand between the stop sign
and an outdoor pool, veiled in blue
tarps, highway at my back.
Can you see my bones
stretch to meet
the torn sky? I want

to be a man,
forget my womb
ever held tiny fingers
in its palm, my spine
swayed like snow,
pinning the pines'
thinned arms down.

For My Son: A Forest of Stars

After Ocean Vuong

Before
we give up our country to give you
a country of your own. You can't have

my eyes, but we'll speak
with the same tongue.
        Someday,

you'll hear sand in my voice
when searching for what is lost

onshore. I want you to have the truth,
but truth is as seductive as a storm

settling over the earth. Many nights,
my mother cried in another room.
I heard lashing. I saw fire—

how scalded skin, to some, is
        love. I hope you don't need to pray

for cinderblock walls. For the sky's colours to steal
our words. You can't yet know

that men can be bent
like branches. That women must kneel
too often, their eyes on the red shore

behind. There is a moment when I touch you
and you are real, not a shadow

of shed skin as we turn to dust
on the hardwood. If you go somewhere
without me, my face candling

into melted wax, you must understand—I fell
in love while we were falling, the devil

wind tearing at my mouth and nose.
All I could do was smile.

When you step away, look
at the ground I've given you. Dig

until your shovel hits
the trees' twisted roots, spring

water gurgling below. This is the proof:
our hands on these shafts,

my words held in your mouth
     like stars that forget

          they have to fall.

girl, unfinished

You wish you didn't have a name. You wish
he didn't bring flowers,

a casserole—his tires rutting the gravel
driveway, the morning

police came to say your father died. Silence
& grief. Branches bent
under the snow. Silence
like a wound

in your brother's mouth. The scent
of cedar: a memory

chest, cushioned pews, trees
behind the church. Silence
& snow. But he was there, with his wife,
before your mother was his

wife. Then, his cigarettes, flicked
on the lawn. Summer,

caught in your throat. He
took your clothes, changed the locks, left you
in the yard. Silence

all around—hungry sky,
a broken tricycle rusting

the sidewalk, front wheel
twisted. Then, the wings
your skin grew over

as you stood wishing
for a second bloom.

Wedding Dress

In the back of my mother's closet,
it hangs: a cloud, the vapour
from our lungs the night
we met. Snow
covered this town like a shroud. I imagine
its silk in the half-moon
light, dirt scarring delicate seams,
the dusty floor. The way we smiled,
standing in the July heat. I slid thin fabric
past my hips afterwards, abandoned
to a hanger, the space
above an old .22. Perhaps
a dress is only silk and lace. A sweetheart
neckline, the varying whiteness
of its bones. Shut away
there, the corset gapes, tulle
browned with age, as it waits
for warmth—to know the moment
when winter turns to spring
and it will be able to twirl
in the floor-length mirror, light
and new and impossible to harm.

Revenant

I want the river to live
in shades of chalk
and moon, bones

on its bed. I see it clearly
in my mind, yet it hides itself
there, alongside the street

with a green house where my parents
lived. Great pines resting their heads
against the sky. The colours

at dawn, sweet chill in the summer
grass before early snows. When I return,
the water is no longer

hidden. Its teeth bear down
on the banks. But I notice only
how low it sits in the mouth

of the gorge, an unforgiving pull
at my ankles—the way it rushes forth
to become something else.

The Gulf

Rain refuses to stop falling
        as if it can dissolve all things—
a road, its name. Inside my belly,
   another belly, burning. Small
       hands change shape in the dark
night. Can I give you tomorrow
   when I've lost hold of today? A man lays next to me,
   sweltering, and I'm stupid
with the need to be small. To reduce my body
       to a war. For you to crawl headfirst into
the fanged mouth
   of this world, abandoned
on the gravel roadside in a storm-surge. I forget
           not to sacrifice my bones like gods
make a woman forget praise
   without suffering. Still, the sky
       can't be outrun. A hurricane sweeps
   sand and sea, bodies torn
away from the nearest shore. Shouldn't one rest
upon the other? Darling child, show me
         why I swell, your name
   cut from fire. That you are
       not crawling, but running headlong
into your own skin. When you get here,
show me the sky—
         the earth's skin
as changed as our own
       by sea levels, a sharpening storm.

In My Father's Voice

It wasn't pain that surfaced
when you knew we were listening. How
you were made to quit
school in eighth grade, heavy
machinery in your hands
on the side of a half-built mountain
dam. The stutter when my mother

asked you to sign anything. It wasn't the pen,
but your fingers, fumbling, the shape
of letters you couldn't find. There

was no accent from the old country—
Ukrainian you spoke on the farm,
your father and two siblings buried
by a creek, the red barn's bones
cracked under the sun. You never mentioned

your plans, or your struggle—
                    how the sky hung
so low, you were crippled. Only
that I could find water
in every wood. That the pines
would grow tall enough to
pierce the sky. But, at night, I still hear

            muffled cries through the walls—
how a man on his knees sounds
like lightning. How the door echoes
long after it closes. I want

more than anything, now, to tell you
I understand, mouth bent to my son's
small ear—what it took to quiet
   cries born of hunger, of the cold
       night on your skin.

The Afternoon I Was Abandoned, Sparrows

flew into the yard. It was spring, but cold. The man
changing the locks while I stood in the street
was a man my mother knew. Like powder, wings

>   raised above fresh snow. Like arms
>   swarming the walls of a house, they flew
>   into the horizon's long frame. The man

turned his back, closed the door
when he finished. But the sparrows sat
on the snow-laden lawn, refusing

>   shelter. Refusing to flee white fire. Their wings,
>   beating the air, spread like small
>   crosses racing over the ground.

Winter in Sodertalje

Not even a street light. Forgotten,

a baby lays on the floor,
bald and screaming. I dig out the car,
haul wood. At one point,
I turn, looking for proof in disappearing
prints. With the sky
in shards, who will notice if I am lost?

In the bed, my arms spoon
a pillow, old imprint of your face
clinging to blue cotton. I don't ask you
to name this silence
when you appear, bedraggled and beaten,
winter woven inside moon-pale skin. Instead, I build
a fire in each hearth, large enough
to burn through the black

night. In sleep, you reach for me,
a spruce to a stark sky, aching
limbs sheathed with snow.

As the Daughter Recites Psalm 91

He says he'll kill her

if she runs, but she doesn't
run. She sits still, deep

inside the planet
of her bathtub, water
roaring in place

of her mouth. Maybe
it's for the sound. Maybe it's a wish
to pour herself into another
body, release the parts

grown soft. She bares her skin
to cold, white tile,
soaking wounds in Epsom
salts, purpling
like foxgloves. Here,

she can close her eyes
and forget she's a mother.
How his mouth in her ear sounds
like penitence. That she still longs
his fingers on her skin
as soon as the water

cools. I stand outside, my hands
pressed to the door
in surrender, as I once slept,

unfinished, in the cradle
of her bones. Yet,
in my mouth, a prayer:

this time, let her not forget.

Hiraeth

Pine-rimmed water, winding
highway, heaving skies. You slipped
your skin like an old housedress,
humid summer nights we were alone.
Left it, pooling the cream rug
in your bedroom. West,
the sky rested on the shoulders of mountains,
and I lost my breath as we climbed
over rock, dirty stumps,
soft with decay. Deep inside a twisted wood,
water we could only hear
breathed cool air on our damp skin.
I was lost then too.
Why have you shown me
ragged ridges, a river,
if they weren't mine to keep?
Tonight, somewhere else,
the sky bends over my face,
pink lace, low clouds.
I want to be a lodgepole
pine, planted in the ruins
of a logged peak,
head straining
to touch the tilted sky.

Autumn Wars

I wait to see how we'll leave
    paradise. Queen palms

sway over porticos and porches. Our small sons
sleep surrounded by treed slopes they
              may not remember. We are

long miles from childhood, the cold north we fled. Why
do we always want better? Is rising
not enough? I blanket you

against this new season, long-tendriled limbs
curled into commas, the wind crowing. Perhaps

we should be less like the pines we've left
to petrify, roots stifled in frozen ground. Less like

                  whispers of dogwood
blossoms that never peek through snow
banks, that never claw

through my mother's thinned voice
calling me home. You are the only place
I come back to. The sun,
            perishing in a storm

can't be seen amidst the rain, the same way
it can't survive the snow's white

mask. Once, we armed ourselves and drove
over tundra in a twining womb
                          of white fields and sky

to get out. I saw then that some things can never be
                made beautiful.

Current

   I ask if we're still
friends, our second child between us
in the bed. Spent,

someone I can't dream has left
this body, a cathedral squandered
where mountains fall flat at our feet. I look back
on ruins, the sky galaxying south, always

   pulling away from the earth
as if it knows better. Suffering is faithful
work. We kneel, our mouths

closer to the ground than the sky. Maybe
our child is the window
and we are merely walls. Our parents have been
lost to us like rainfall is lost
to the dry earth in drought, red sun

bleeding in brushstrokes. This house is
a wild forest now. There is no city. Reaching for pine
trees in your steel-dark eyes, the taste of

rain in your mouth, I begin
the dutiful act of drowning
in everything not yet lost

        like water.

Burning

Because you used to be
made of winter: snow

and cold and sleet. Because their hands
let go and you tired of freezing. Because

you're building yourself
from fire—secrets

are only safe when someone is
underground. You were a woman running

until you forgot you were
a woman. The fire, nailed inside you

like a sword. Why would a child make you less
than the horses, saddled

next to the barn? Their reins
dangle and, yet—. I once saw fire

spread through a swamp
during a storm, after lightning

struck. It's not restraint
that is feared, but being left

to burn. How a fire can
starve, surrounded by air.

Elegy for My Child

It didn't take long for you
to go missing. I roll over
and tap the window. Each fat whisker
of rain stains the glass black,
a skinny-streamed feather. Once,
your body was so small
we couldn't wrap you tight enough
in a blanket. How you howled to return
to a womb. Sometimes, when pregnant, I wondered
how long I could hold you inside
before my skin's heft would falter.

What do I do with this rain
drilling the roof like nails into planks?

I'd gladly give up this night,
close my eyes to forget your cries
are an ocean. This ache isn't
the ache I imagine when I think about losing you
in the grocery store, running madly
between aisles, shallow panes, registers. Outside,

the house cranes its neck
into the sky, wind hurling itself
against the frame. It shudders,
body stripped bare, standing
empty to face the street.

It's in the fall—

The way the fork
clatters to the empty plate. An open hand
to ruined skin. How snow
can't help but reach
for the ground, too heavy to pretend
to fly. How will we leave each other

next? Unfasten the clouds—
lend them to the earth. Let us lie
on our backs, the winter

night rising around us. Could we fly
if nothing before had fallen? Imagine

every petal, water droplet, everything
that was once part of the sky,
surging like the sun
from the horizon. Yet these hands,

lined with ghosts: rivers, children,
your bare skin—they still fall
like snow. Next to you,

I wait for the wreck, two cars
on a one lane road. For the wind
to pick up. In your hands,
to be perfectly ruined.

Nocturne

I can't see the whole sky
at once. Black-ribboned water
churning across the lake. Pines behind

mountain peaks. When the sun lowers
its jaw to the earth, I finally know
how to disappear. Shadow-flames

flicker, the way I remember your voice. The moon's
husk is already bright, but distant. It won't come
into focus, the way stubble blurred your chin

in my fingers. I replay how I failed
to make you love me. The hours it takes
to know darkness. As night arrives,

instead of folding myself in its chest
like a child, I sit on the porch and listen
to wind in the leaves, squirrels foraging,

the water baying at large rocks
on riverbanks. I remember
when we were tethered to light

like flies. But I can't see
the whole sky at once. How bright
the bodies it holds.

The Windsurfer

My husband is made of cloth, the sea
staining his skin with salt
as it exhales. Pale, he's used
to falling from the sky, wings
tangled in the wind. Each tear
is sewn shut by deft hands
and yet, his skin is threadbare,
dragged over rocks onshore
when he makes his descent. Like an arrow,
I draw a needle across the wounds,
waiting for the skin to give, the night
too perilous to excise, to run from. As long
as he's made to fly without being able to see
the ground, I learn how to glide, to tread
water. But, we're never freer than
when we're falling. Death, take me
first, the wind in every hollow. I'm not afraid
of the sound a body makes
when it dips below sea level. I fear
steering the stretched sky alone, wind
tearing through space
he's left like a song
to hang the hungry sea.

The Conversation

Bones shatter against a hull's open
mouth. I crane to see beyond
fists flinging me down, brute
breaths trapped behind bared teeth

like the clasped tines of a zipper.
You cut me out of a lace dress:
slit of skin, as the knife fangs

from tail to throat, a still-waving rainbow
trout fresh from white waters.

Would you take my head, too,
if you could?

Belly emptied black
into billowing water, you lay me down,
carcasses collecting like rinds
along the banks' soft lips.

Remove my womb, the poppy
red eggs, my stacked spine's silver

boning. I can't be a man any more
than you can wrest the slim waist
of a cloud. Maybe,

before the blade sinks, you let
go, a memory of pretty bones blistering
the ribbon of your pink throat.

I'll swim upstream through a sky of water,
gather myself in the river's palm.

Hands, I've Had

To disappear, I close the front door
on my mother, as a man's hands thrash
worn yellow walls. The winter

sun, heavy-lidded, hangs
halfway over our house until the night sky appears,
star-shot, holes where its eyes should be.

How I long for blindness, the sky
holding itself above.

&

Maybe, I didn't see you
until a gasp of tires, black
ice-slick highway, the truck's tail-

spin. Your arm shot
across my chest like a brick
barrier. Before the meridian met steel.

Sometimes we're still sliding,
a prairie sky crouched overhead.

Sometimes, there is only falling:
fingers clasping steel like snow.

&

Tonight, we're still
breathing. Your hand cleaves
     to the skin under my shirt, a cigarette

cupped in the other. The moon
bares its teeth, swallows
     the dark. We sit on the deck,

kids sleeping in the bowels behind
us. I imagine falling, clothes
     strewn on your parent's floor. I'm afraid, bare-

skinned. Our bodies break
the wind, another war
     whittling us down. Your hands,

like pink-tipped lilies, are the only things
pinning me to the earth,
     proof in disappearing prints.

Winter in Florida

Tracks in the snow sing
somewhere else, the cicadas
singing beyond our back porch

tonight. You're heavy-lidded,
legs kicked out in front of a lawn
chair. The light, always changing—

do you see? I sit so still
but my eyes are open. Maybe
north, we would at least leave

tracks. Is this a better world I hear
singing, as we wait, withering
in the southern heat? December,

trapped in our throats. Either way,
there's no going back—can't you
see? Look quickly: the sun

dives behind a swamp. Behind
the house. Behind, voices
colour the wind. But it's you I want

to sing us away now, swallow
to a spring morning. We've been lost in
a string of seasons, in every sky.

Holding the Sky

It isn't night that draws us
apart. Nor burials: our small bodies

up to our necks
in snow. We left those children there,

fair-haired and fat-fingered,
dreaming of spring, daisy fields

behind our old green house. Even now,
you run as if you can't help it. Tonight,

I find you, skin pinned and prodded, pupils
nailed down to a prick. I drape myself in heavy clothes

as if it will keep you warm. As smoke wafts
from your mouth into the night

sky. I try to run my fingers through it,
but it changes as it leaves

your body, and I am left
with only this, brother:

dusk rippling in front of us,
my empty hands.

When My Mother and I Speak about the Weather

She holds a knife
to the apple's skin, green
and smooth. The veins

in her hands raise. I keep trying to
forget that she wants to open
my body like a constellation. To disassemble

the stars. She gestures with the tip
toward my neck, a slit of mirror. It catches
light from the windows. I want

to remind her that the light outside
can be anything she wants. But, she can't reach
the stars. And so. There is nothing else

to do, except open the sky's chest
and let the stars fall
like seeds, like so much debris.

Live Oaks

languish amid parcels of land,
pink and tan houses. I should know

paradise, but all I see, sometimes,
are the forests I knew before, covered in snow

as we waited for the thaw, for pines
to spread their arms under

   the white sun. Like horses
waiting in the stables, I ran

in the spring—longing a body's weight
against me, longing to run

free. In Florida, the ground sinks wet
under my feet. The sun, heavy

on the oaks' backs. I don't know
if I dreamed other places now. If

the trees I once knew
survived as I survived—-

   hoping not to be cut down
   young, needing nothing more than light

rain, the night
       to part ways with the sky.

In Hindsight

You slept with your fists
balled next to your ears,

as if you had to fight
   even then. I wanted you

like rainfall that wouldn't subside. Your father
belonged less to me than to you

afterwards. Perhaps that's true of us
   both. But he became a face

on a flyer, posted on wooden poles
strung with wire.   Some days, I imagine you

on the banks of a river, wet with white-
water-numbed limbs. You deserve

to hear the gurgle in its throat, before
it dries up in the sun

scalding your shoulders. Some days,
I come into focus: my head

in your neck, my hands
     in your hands. When I fade

with the cicadas, sing for me. Tell me
   all of this is an accident—you are not

my body's ruin, but the ocean
I empty myself into.

Any Other Sun

Long seconds your leaving sews
in my skin: a daughter's gasp, trapped
in the space between bodies. The map unfurls

and I keep running. What is it I hope to find? A war
breaks out in this borrowed home
as I recline in the Gulf's clean palm, adrift

under the sun. Tell me I'm not
a disappointment. The struggle
to get to this country. You couldn't even read.

I wish I could carry you now, as your mother did,
show you this world. This world,
a churning river. In the morning, a child can be

almost grown. How would it have been
inside your skin, your language
lapping the shores of these shallow bones? I saw snow

crowning silver sills. I saw you disappear
like the sun. Here, my hands belong
to someone. Thin, like my mother's

blood. I'm ready to be powerless against
the night. To leave behind skin
pinned beneath my palms like sheets
on a line, swaying in a southern wind.

Notes

"Little Hell." The title references a song by City and Colour.

"On Nights when I Am a Mother." This poem is loosely after Pablo Neruda's "Funeral in the East" and "Walking Around" and Tomas Tranströmer's "Prelude."

"Hit and Run." This poem is after Kevin Prufer's "Fallen from a Chariot."

"Athena." This poem references a line from Ocean Vuong's "Telemachus."

"For My Son: A Forest of Stars." References a poem by Ocean Vuong called "To My Father / To My Future Son."

"Hiraeth." (Welsh) ". . . a homesickness for a home you cannot return to, or that never was."—Oxford and Merriam-Webster

"Current." The last line references a poem by Meg Day called "San Francisco / October 17, 1989."

"Nocturne." This poem is after Chloe Honum's "Come Back" and loosely follows the form there, mirroring some language.